Endurance Riding and Trekking

Text and illustrations by Sally Bell
Designed and typeset by Alan Hamp
Cover photograph: Eric G Jones

A catalogue record of this book is available from
the British Library

ISBN 0-900226-54-4

The Pony Club
Allander House
NAC Stoneleigh Park
Kenilworth
Warwickshire CV8 2RW ·
Code: 01203. Tel: 698300 Fax: 696836

Printed and bound in England
by Westway Offset, Wembley

Contents

Introduction

What is Endurance Riding?

It is about excitement.

It is about riding a pony who is fit for the job, carrying a rider who is light and well-balanced in the saddle over all sorts of ground.

It is about a rider who can find the route over challenging terrain, read the map correctly and bring the pony in at the end of the ride still fit and healthy enough to go on.

It is the challenge of true horsemanship.

It is not a race.

Endurance riding requires true horsemanship. It is possible to be a flaw-less equestrian rider but know little of the horse. It takes a great deal of skill and judgement to ride a horse many miles in a single day. You should be in complete harmony with your horse.

Endurance riding is about covering a given distance in a given time, fol-lowing maps and markers and using your skill to bring your horse home in the best possible condition. It may be a tough sport but it has the wel-fare of the main participant – the horse – as the key consideration.

It is about riding a pony who is fit for the job.

A major factor of the sport is that the horse's condition is carefully monitored throughout the event.

It tests the fitness of the horse. You'll have to make sure that he is fit enough not to suffer from strained tendons or ligaments; that he won't get out of breath up steep hills or from a lot of trotting; that his heart can pump the blood round at a nice steady beat – he must be fit enough to compete.

In endurance riding you compete against yourself. By riding within the limits of age, fitness and riding ability anyone can do it. Yes, there are winners, but it isn't always the fastest who wins. Improving the recovery rate after each ride gives a great deal of satisfaction and encouragement to 'non-competitive' riders. So by competing within the parameters of type, age, soundness, toughness and ability, any horse can do it.

The motto 'To finish is to win' sums up the whole thing.

1
History

Modern endurance riding started in the United States in 1955 when a group of riders set out to prove that modern horsemen had not forgotten how to ride long distances and yet bring horses home fit to go further. The travelled the old Pony Express routes over the Sierra Nevada – 100 miles of rocky trails, from the snow line down to deep canyons along the old Western States Trail now accepted as the toughest ride in the world. The famous Tevis Cup is still ridden along this route every year. Horses have to carry a total of 11½ stone and the first ten horses home carrying that weight are judged for best condition.

In 1966, Tom Quilty launched a 100-mile ride in the Blue Mountains of Sydney, Australia. Steep mountains, quicksands, drops and hills made up this incredibly tough trail. The ride is now held at various similar venues across Australia.

Britain cannot offer the spectacular climbs and descents of these two countries, but 'The Golden Horseshoe', held on Exmoor each year tests

'Cougar Rock'
Western States Trail.

the fitness and endurance of riders who cover 50 miles on each of the two days. The 'Summer Solstice' one-day endurance race covers 100 miles – the placings are decided on time, but the horse must have passed the veterinary inspection.

Today, endurance competitions are judged on the condition of the horse at the finish compared with his condition at the start. All of these rides are run under strict veterinary control to protect the horse. In less enlightened days at the end of the last century, huge money was won and lost on distance 'races' and 'trials' where many animals ended up dead. Now endurance riding is entirely based on the condition and welfare of the horse, which may be 'spun' (withdrawn) from the ride by the vets at any time.

The Pony Club introduced endurance riding as one of its disciplines in 1997. It is a sport which, at this level, can be enjoyed by any rider and is a great introduction to many years of pleasure and partnership with your horse.

2
Preparation

Endurance riding is about fitness. Your pony must be fit for the job and you must be fit, too. Endurance is not about racing or just getting there faster than the next person. It is all about riding skill, knowing your horse's ability, and using this knowledge to present him at the final vetting with a low pulse, an un-bruised mouth and a flowing, sound trot-up for the vet, with both of you feeling that you could go on for a few more miles.

How many times have you heard it said that riders just sit on top an enjoy themselves while the horses do all the work? How many timers have you been really tired after a long ride or a hard lesson? As you get more tired you become heavier, less able to maintain a good balance and less capable of lightening the load. Eventually your concentration goes and you end up riding on 'auto-pilot', which is when things can go wrong.

You don't need to be super-fit but you do need to be able to get off and jog along with your horse – to stretch your legs and ease his back over long distances. The going underfoot will be easier for your horse

Jogging down a rough place.

to cope with if you are off his back, letting him balance himself and pick his way down a steep, stony track. Take the reins over his head and give him enough length to balance himself. Too tight and he will not be able to balance himself and will rely on you to hold him up – probably walking on your toes – and you will be more of a hindrance than a help to him. It is possible to go faster down a rough place jogging beside your horse than sitting on his back. All this means that you have to be fit enough not to get out of breath, not to get a 'stitch' in your side, and for your legs not to feel like lead.

You need to be able to ride as lightly and well balance as possible, going forwards easily at the trot and not rising too high out of the saddle, which wastes energy. Have your stirrups at a comfortable length. You need to be able to mount lightly – so as not to jolt your horse's back muscles – and not to have to 'mountaineer' up into the saddle. A bit of patience teaching your horse to stand still saves a lot of time and temper on the trail. It is bad manners for him to shoot off as soon as your foot is in the stirrup or your seat in the saddle, as well as being potentially dangerous. Good manners can save precious seconds.

Tiredness can be caused by not having an adequate meal. Don't skip breakfast because you are too excited to eat. You are going to need all that high energy fuel. Take something in your pocket or bag – not chocolate which doesn't travel well in the heat or bananas which get squashed. Dried fruit, marzipan or a muesli type bar are good. Make sure you drink plenty of fluids to avoid getting thirsty and to prevent the possibility of dehydration.. The squashy packs of sports drinks are worth finding space for, as you often only need a few sips.

How fit?
Whatever the size of your horse or pony he must be fit for the job. We will presume that he is in regular work and that you ride every weekend, either hacking out or having a lesson, and probably at least once during the week for a short period. Winter riding may include hunting, and summer will entail rallies and competition as well as riding out with friends.

If you hunt during the winter or lead an active, competitive summer, your horse will be fairly fit anyway. The mileages you are likely to ride when you start endurance are unlikely to stress this kind of animal.

If you are not able to ride sufficiently often to keep the weight off a grass-fed pony in the summer, you must give very serious thought to just how much you can ask of him. Most ponies tend to put on weight at an alarming rate once the grass comes through. It is not fair, safe, sensible or kind to make an overweight, un-toned animal compete in a sport for which he is not prepared. Many ponies suffer from a combination of obesity and over-enthusiasm, unable to know when they have had enough. They could, literally, go on until they drop.

If you intend to compete, you will have to plan an exercise and feeding schedule in advance. An overweight animal is a recipe for disaster: extra strain is put on heart and lungs, and tendons can break down with the increase in the workload.

Getting really fit can't be done in odd days here and there. Legs need to be hardened by steady, slow work built up over a period of time, and lungs and heart strengthened the same way so that they can stand the stress put on them under competition, whether it is jumping, gymkhana or endurance. Unfit muscles lead to a greater likelihood of damage and this applies to the rider as well as to the horse, so aim to get fit together. Plenty of active walking to toughen bones and tendons, steady trotting up hills and a little cantering to activate lungs and heart for the horse and jogging alongside for you should help get both of you in trim.

Aim to get fit together.

Because of the variety of ponies it is impossible to make hard and fast rules for the length of time and miles covered on exercise or how long it will take a certain animal to reach a particular peak of fitness. The naturally athletic type finds it easier to attain a good fitness level with little effort, while the heavier native breeds, or those already overweight and the less forward-going animals can present a real challenge. It is up to the rider to devise a fittening programme based on personal knowledge of the particular pony or to seek advice from a riding instructor who knows the animal.

• *Hint: If you are starting from scratch your programmes should include a session of one to one and a half hours exercise two or three times a week for six weeks, riding at walk and trot. Follow this by a further six weeks, but include cantering.*

• *Once a week measure your horse's heart rate with a stethoscope (more about this further on) after you have had a brisk canter for about quarter of a mile. The quicker his heart rate returns to its natural level the fitter he is becoming.*

• *The usual resting heart rate will be between 32 and 44 beats per minute – make sure you know what his normal heart rate is when at rest in the stable. Keeping a training log is a sensible way to check on progress.*

You should aim to be able to maintain a steady but active trot for several miles and be fit enough to ride lightly and in balance, taking as little energy out of yourself and your horse as possible. Endurance riding is about saving energy, landing less heavily in the saddle and saving your horse's back. You should be agile enough to get on easily and your mount should be obliging enough to stand still while you do so.

Girth and back areas need to be tough enough to withstand having the saddle (and you) on them for a long time. Applying witch-hazel or white spirit is the traditional way of toughening up the soft areas, but gradually building up the fitness and condition of the horse is utterly essential.

No foot no horse – so take care of hooves both inside and out by correct feeding or additives to promote good hoof growth, and a hoof preparation to keep the outer horn in good condition. The importance of regular and correct shoeing and foot care goes without saying.

There are no short cuts to getting you both fit, but once you attain a reasonable level of fitness it takes very little effort to sustain it, as long as you know the physical capabilities of both you and your mount so you can enjoy your ride.

As well as physical fitness you have to have the right mental attitude to want to ride for miles. If you get bored after an hour's hack and you don't like being wet, cold, hot, tired or thirsty, perhaps you are looking at the wrong sport. Endurance includes all of these and more. It is about getting to know your horse; knowing how he feels about his partnership with you and how you feel about yours with him. You need to know when he should ease up for his own good, and at the same time know how far you can push him under the pressure of competition.

If you don't like being wet, perhaps you are looking at the wrong sport.

Endurance riding will improve your horsemanship, your understanding of horses and your riding ability as you combine all three to compete safely and successfully. It is a great adventure of discovery about yourself, your horse and the country around you.

Feeding

Feeding is covered in detail in the Pony Club *Manual of Horsemanship*. Many endurance riders use supplements and energisers that can cause some normally sensible animals to go right off the rails, with disastrous results to themselves and their riders. Anything used should be treated with caution, as directions usually refer to horses and not smaller animals. Always read the label. Manufacturers are there to help, so if in doubt, ask them. The day of the ride is not the time to try a new feed or supplement.

You will find that endurance riding is a sport at the cutting edge in that top competitors will look carefully into, and experiment with, the latest theories and practices on modern feedstuffs.

Many endurance horses, for example, are fed alfalfa and chop as part of their diet, which retains moisture within the gut and helps combat dehydration. It is valuable to pick up tips such as this from experienced fellow competitors, but the main point to remember is that sensible feeding, following the standard, long practised rules of good horsemanship should suffice.

13

3

What Kind of Horse?

The Pony Club has four categories of ride. The MERLIN RIDE is 5 miles long at a speed of 5.5 to 8 mph: the KESTREL RIDE is 10 miles long at a speed of 6.5 to 8 mph: the OSPREY RIDE is 20 miles at a speed of 6.5 to 8 mph and the EAGLE RIDE, 30 miles at a speed of 7 to 8 mph. These distances and speeds are well within the scope of most family ponies and horses. However, some are better suited to endurance than others.

Size and Type

Let us start with the smallest ponies whose riders are of an age and ability to compete safely. Welsh ponies are renowned for their enthusiasm and stamina and will still be giving their owners a good ride when stirrups have gone down a lot of holes over the years. They are also nimble and surefooted over difficult terrain. At lower levels, Welsh cobs and cob crosses will perform well even if they haven't the smooth flowing paces of the Arab types. If the horse has a lot of up-and-down movement he may be wasting energy and can be a wearing ride. However, a gassy, pulling, over-excited Arab can be an even worse proposition. You must feel comfortable on the horse and that means being happy to ride him

Some are better suited to endurance riding than others.

over demanding ground where you know you can trust him to be an equal partner, who will not take the upper hand nor leaving all the work up to you. You should not have to ride with your heart in your mouth – this is supposed to be fun! The horse or pony must be physically capable to carry out the job without due strain, and an animal that is well put-together, of good conformation, will do this more easily than one with a straight shoulder and upright pasterns which lack shock absorption.

Horses must be over four years old to compete. Older horses can take part in endurance rides, and compete well at a suitable level; they are past the age of splints, and anything that was going to develop has usually done so. The odd lump and bump may be unsightly but takes nothing off his performance. He has also seen the world and will take being an endurance horse in his stride, happily enjoying the attentions of his adoring crew.

The mental outlook of a prospective endurance horse should not be under-estimated. A calm, laid-back sort of horse will have a low pulse rate and not get stewed up on the ride and will vet at the finish with the minimum of crewing. he will be a joy to handle even if he doesn't go like the wind. The beautiful, highly strung, physically perfect pony may have a screw missing. He may be unable to take the pressure of other ponies coming up behind (or even on the horizon), without the overwhelming need to be in front of everyone all the time. It is possible for him to be on such a high at the end of the ride, however

There are special awards from Breed Societies.

carefully you have tried to bring him in, that his mental attitude to crewing, the hustle and bustle and the pure excitement of all that running may keep his pulse too high. However, it can take a year for a horse to settle to endurance so don't give up too soon if this is the horse you love.

Although there are plenty of theories on what breed or cross makes the perfect endurance horse, it is accepted that the toughness and thriftiness of our native breeds crossed with the stamina, quality of bone and agility of the Arab and the speed of the English Thoroughbred produces the kind of horse that usually succeeds. There are not hard and fast rules. The most unlikely horse pops up from time to time and becomes an outstanding endurance horse despite his size and type, Several breed societies give awards for performance in endurance as it all helps to promote the prowess of their particular breed.

Above all - whatever size or shape your endurance horse is he must be sound and have the ability to carry the job through. He must have the right mental attitude to do the job and he must be right for you. Just remember to ride within the abilities of both your horse and yourself.

4
Equipment

Most endurance groups with which you ride will have some form of tack check. The purpose of this is to ensure that your tack is safe for the job. The stitching on stirrup leathers or reins must be sound, leatherwork must be in good condition and all tack should fit and be well adjusted. Make sure that it is clean and presents a good, workmanlike impression.

Standards and requirements of dress and equipment vary. For Pony Club requirements see the official publication *Correct Dress for Riders*. Other groups have no such requirements, only insisting that your hat and footwear meet their safety standards.

Looking at the wider field of endurance riding, you will find that equipment for horse and rider is designed for safety, comfort and ease of maintenance, whilst still allowing a certain amount of individuality.

The Rider's Gear

In endurance you are riding for a long time. Comfortable clothes that give you freedom of movement to ride, mount and dismount easily and which are also suitable for the weather conditions are important. Standards of dress acceptable in other countries cause consternation among some British traditionalists.

Your hat must be of the correct standard. Endurance societies have a different standard from the Pony Club, allowing lightweight, ventilated hats to be worn. Pony Club approved headwear (see *Correct Dress for Riders*) is acceptable to these societies but not the other way round, so make sure you are wearing the right hat.

Underwear may not be the first thing you think about, but after several miles of hard riding you may wish that you had given more attention to it. Cotton with Lycra for stretch is better than Nylon. You also need a comfortable top and extra layers, depending on the weather. Should you have to pull out of the course and stop, because of lameness or an accident or to help another rider, you can very quickly get chilled. If it is raining as well, the situation can become serious unless you have

17

Endurance gear for horse and rider.

brought a waterproof tied on to the back of the saddle. (Your crew should have a spare sweatshirt in their kit for you) Experienced riders, who should know better, have been known to set off under grey skies in short-sleeved T-shirts only to find that the heavens have opened and they are suddenly suffering from hypothermia. British weather is notorious for its unpredictability. Not only can you suffer from chill winds, but a sleeveless top may leave you unbearably burnt by the sun and wind or scratched by branches along the route. Dress sensibly.

Many endurance riders now wear riding tights in preference to jodphurs. These padded tights are made in cotton Lycra and stretch to fit without wrinkles as well as having no seams to cause rubbing. They originated in the USA and come in a variety of colours to co-ordinate with the rest of your gear and that of your horse. Whatever you decide to ride in, make sure that you are going to be comfortable for a long time.

Half-chaps with short boots or riding trainers (not fashion or sports trainers) that have a heel, are comfortable and practical. You may need to get off and jog with your horse, so remember that boots with smooth soles are slippery on wet hillsides. You can make just as smart an appearance wearing the latest endurance gear as you can wearing a more traditional outfit. Remember to dress for comfort and safety. If you carry a stick it must be under 30" (75cm).

You will need a map-case (a clear, waterproof plastic case on a cord), to hold ride instructions and your map. As mapcases tend to flap, tie themselves in a knot round your neck or get caught on branches you must make sure that the cord is long enough for you to fit over your shoulder and carry the case snugly under your arm. Stuffing your map-case down the front of your shirt is not a comfortable alternative.

It is important to carry a drink. You can attach a special drink holder to your saddle which takes a plastic drink container with a top you pull up with your teeth.

It is also wise, and in some cases obligatory, to take a first aid kit. Contents of this should include a triangular bandage, a wound dressing, a veterinary bandage, glucose type sweets, a survival bag (a special foil sheet which folds up to a pack about 4" by 6" or 10cms by 15 cms), a hoof pick and a whistle. Check the rules of the event as to what you will need. Sometimes it is possible to hire a first aid kit on deposit at the event – but always check. It is certainly a useful addition to your standard riding equipment and may be carried in a 'bum bag' by the rider.

No sensible distance rider will leave home without some sort of 'spare hoof' for the horse. Nothing is more guaranteed to spoil a good ride than a lost shoe. At present there are two kinds of emergency horse footwear. First, an 'Equiboot' type– a heavy hoof-shaped unit tightened with a spring clip. These are used in the USA for continuous riding in 100-mile competitions, rather than shoes. However they can be tricky to fix and need a certain amount of strength and knack to fit them properly. The alternative type originated as a poultice boot and is called a 'Shoof'. This is lighter in construction, easier to put on and, although not designed for continuous riding will last a 100 miles or more. Both can easily be attached to a 'D' ring on your saddle and may make the difference between winning and losing.

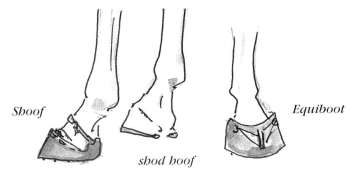

Shoof   *Equiboot*

shod hoof

The other useful item is a simple sponge on a string attached to the saddle. In hot conditions it enables you to make use of any available natural water (streams etc.,) to sponge your horse while he is drinking. Keeping the horse's temperature down will help maintain condition throughout the ride and make it easier for your crew to cool him at checkpoints and at the finish.

Gear for the Horse

Leather tack is a quality item and should be treated as such. It looks smart and with good cleaning and maintenance it will last many years. However, times are changing and synthetic tack is now very popular with endurance riders. Although the Pony Club recommend leather tack, synthetics are allowed but only in traditional colours. At rides organised by the Pony Club for members, coloured equipment is not allowed. Synthetic tack is practical in that it stands a lot of abuse in foul weather and is very tolerant of the amount of water that your crew is likely to get over it. It will rinse out and dry with no harm, whereas leather tack will stiffen and will need loving attention to keep it in good condition.

Bridles, breastplates and martingale attachments can be made of

Combination bridle: the bit unclips and it becomes a headcollar.

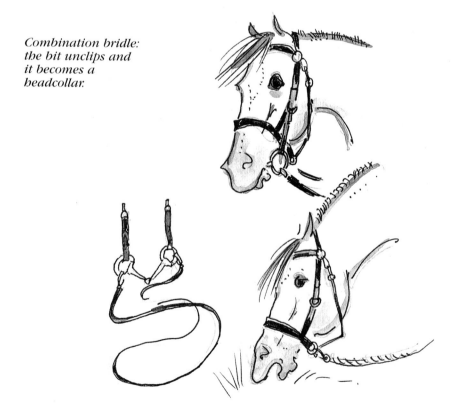

webbing or BioThane. Webbing needs to have sweat washed out of it, whilst BioThane or a similar material with a shiny surface, will just wipe clean. Neoprene or sheepskin protection can be used on sensitive-skinned animals. As well as conventional styles, 'combination' bridles, of which the bit can be removed quickly, leaving just a headcollar, can be a great asset. Reins are clipped on rather than buckled so that you can unclip one side leaving a long line for leading. Breastplates and martingales have a clip which attaches to a 'D' in the centre of the girth to make it easy to remove without having to undo the girth. Girths are sleeved with Neoprene making them easy to wipe over during crewing and less likely to cause friction against the horse.

New concepts in saddle design and fitting enable the horse to travel further distances, and to carry the weight of the rider with less stress than before and to perform to the very best of his ability by freeing the shoulder.

Stirrups are now available which absorb the continual concussion to hip, knee and ankle joints. These are used in conjunction with a caged front because they are quite large and a small foot could slip through.

All of these refinements are not *essential*, but for anyone starting the lower mileages of endurance riding a well fitting saddle and bridle *are* essential and will see you through a disciplines. Bear in mind though, due to the length of time your horse will be carrying both you and a saddle, coupled with his change in shape as he becomes fitter, the correct fit and comfort of the saddle have a direct bearing on his ability to complete the rides in first-rate condition. Never underestimate the damage a poorly fitting saddle can do. An expensive saddle is not a guarantee of a good fit. Always remember that the day of the ride is *not* the time to try out new equipment!

Heart Monitors

These are mainly used by keen, competitive riders competing at high mileage events where they want to continually monitor the heartrate. They are also a great crewing aid. A heart monitor consists of a transmitter slipped under the girth, near where you would use a stethoscope, or under the saddle panels, depending on which type you go for. The receiver can be worn on your wrist or the saddle and gives a digital read-out. It is a great training aid as well as enabling you to learn how your horse performs under various conditions.

Boots and Bandages

You may not present your horse for vetting in boots or bandages, but if you are using them they must be on for 'tack check'. Unless you really

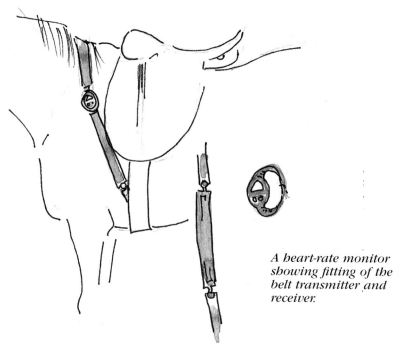

A heart-rate monitor showing fitting of the belt transmitter and receiver.

need them you should consider the risk of small particles of grit or debris getting trapped under them, causing rubbing over a long distance which may give you penalty marks at the final vetting.

Penalty marks at final vetting.

Plaiting

Plaited tails and manes are fine for the show ring but unnecessary for endurance. If you have a horse with a long mane it is a good idea to tidy it up with several long plaits. This helps to keep the neck cool, makes it easier for you to get water down his neck when crewing, and keeps it out of the way of the reins.

If the going is likely to be very muddy and wet and your horse has a long tail you could tape and tie it up out of the way, so that it does not get continually tangled in his legs. It is not a good idea to try this out for the first time on a ride.

Whichever style you decide on, you, you horse and your equipment should present a neat, efficient picture.

5

Paperwork

You have chosen your class, filled in your form and now have received your ride instructions, which include a 'talkround', vet check and start time.

MAP: This will be a copy of the numbered Ordnance Survey map of the area over which you will be riding: probably a black and white one with the route marked in colour; unfortunately, when copied the red often tends to reproduce as a heavy black line which obliterates little details such as contour lines and whether you are riding on a road, track, or in open moorland. Don't forget that steep climbs, downhill sections, hard tracks, soft boggy ground and a lot of gates affect the time it will take you to cover the route. In most cases it is as well to find a colour edition of the relevant map and check the route against it.

TALKROUND: This is a written description of the route that you are to ride. Read it through and match up the written description with the features on the map so that you will recognise where you are going.

> • *Hint: Use a hi-lighter pen to mark special features on the writ-ten description. You can then just glance at the instructions to pinpoint your position. It may say 'go past black barn on the right and follow unmade road to a ford'. Hi-light the words 'black barn' and 'ford' as key points to remember.*

VET SHEET: There will be a veterinary check before you start and at the finish. The style of the sheet may vary but the information needed from you will always be the same. There is a section for you to bring to the vet's attention any blemish, scrape or irregularity of the horse's action. These include old scars or injuries with scabs that might get knocked off, current cuts, overreaches, etc., and lumps and bumps in the saddle and girth area. When you return from the ride and are vetted again, it might be a different vet, so it is essential to produce a written record. The vet may also wish to make some notes. There will be a space

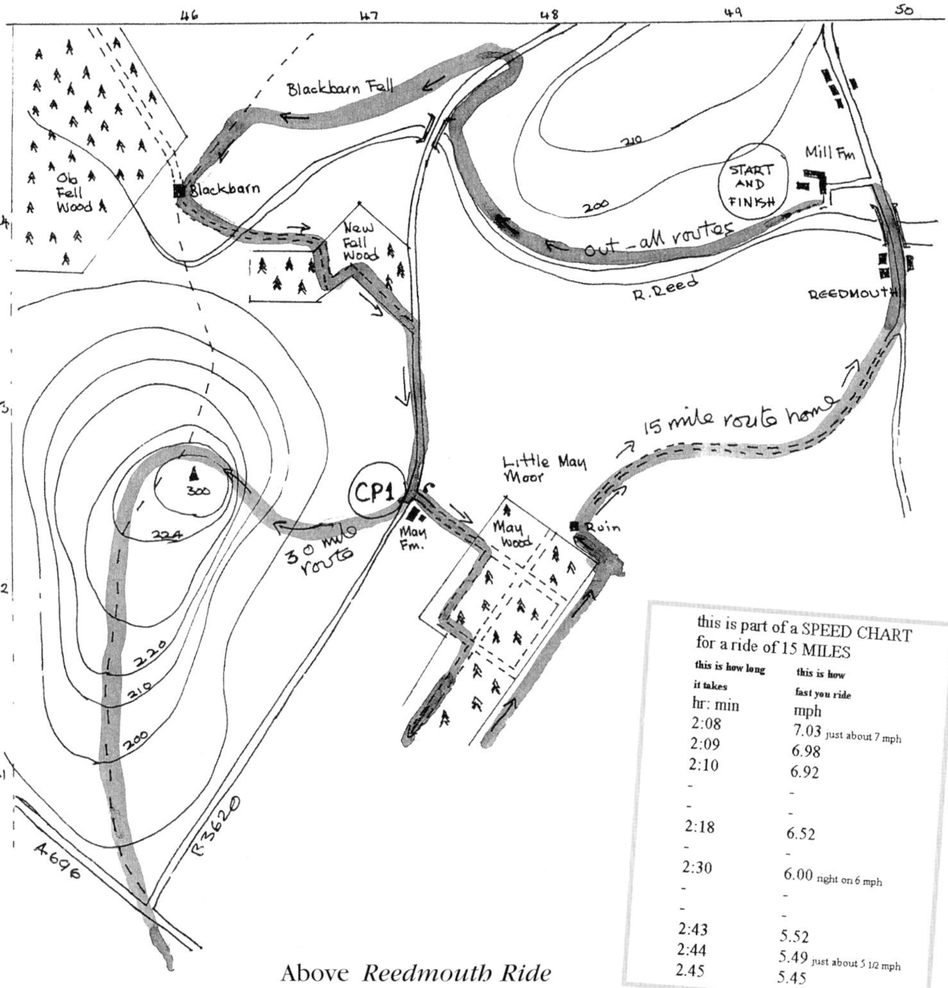

this is part of a SPEED CHART for a ride of 15 MILES

this is how long it takes hr: min	this is how fast you ride mph
2:08	7.03 just about 7 mph
2:09	6.98
2:10	6.92
-	-
-	-
2:18	6.52
-	-
2:30	6.00 right on 6 mph
-	-
-	-
2:43	5.52
2:44	5.49 just about 5 1/2 mph
2.45	5.45

Above *Reedmouth Ride map, and* right, *Talkround.*

for (a) the horse's starting heart-rate, which the vet will fit in, (b) for any mid-way vet check and (c) the finishing rate.

START TIME: Your tack check and start time will also be on the sheet. Make sure that your name, horse's name etc., are filled in. There will also be a section for your final results and any penalties.

Sometimes you will only be asked to trot the horse up, especially if it is a pleasure ride. This is a measure taken to check for any unsoundness before and after the ride.

The vet is not there to vet your horse thoroughly or to find fault with his conformation. He is there to ensure that the horse is fit to complete the ride you have entered on that day.

REEDMOUTH RIDE
O.S.MAP NUMBER .... VENUE: ....

Rider Name......................... Number .... Horse............
Vet Time 9.30   Farrier Time 9.50 Tack Time 10.00   START TIME 10.10

ROUTE MARKING:
orange tape with white flags over open ground.

RIDE INSTRUCTIONS 15 Mile Route.
There is a 3 minute Gate Allowance

From the START turn right out of yard along hard track to gate. Follow riverside track to gate into field. Stay close to wall round field - beware of cattle - to gate on to road. Cross road on to open moorland and follow flags to bridleway. Turn LEFT to Blackbarn then LEFT on to hard track leading to ford. Follow markers to New Fell Wood and down to the road. At road turn RIGHT to CP 1 **(7 miles)**

CAUTION - ROUTES DIVERGE HERE (30 mile route turns RIGHT up over open moorland and steep hill)

15 MILE Route turns LEFT at telephone box up tarmac road to MAY FARM then grass track to woods. Follow markers through woods carefully out on to moor to LITTLE MAY. Turn RIGHT on track then LEFT at Mill Lane back to venue and **FINISH 15 miles.**

Reedmouth Ride Talkround.

Note: If you decide to take up endurance riding and want to compete at 20 miles or more you will need to register your horse and get a log book. This will be where your vet sheets of previous rides will be kept, along with a mastercard of your mileages and results (complete or fail) which will provide the vets and organisers with an accurate record. This is to ensure the well-being of your horse and his ability to complete the miles that you are covering.

SCOTTISH ENDURANCE RIDING CLUB

Entry Details

Type of Ride: Competitive (circled) | Gated

Ride Venue: Ingram

Rider's Name: M. Bell

Speed Category Entered: SC1 (circled) | SC2 | SC3

Thistle Grading Entered: BTQ | BTF | STQ | STF

Bib Number: 2

Distance: 50

Branch: Border

SC1 6-6.99mph, SC2 7-7.99mph, SC1 8+ mph

GT (circled)

Farrier

Signature:

Tack Time: 8 : 45

Signature:

Start Time: 9 : 05.

Finish Time: : :

Time Taken: : :

– Time Allowance: : :

Actual Time Taken: : :

Average Speed:

mph Min speed allowed to achieve mileage is 5.5mph

Competitive Ride Penalties

Competitive Ride Notes:

Time Penalties: 1 penalty for every 2 mins over or under.

Heart Rate Penalties: 1 penalty for every 4 beats over 48 bpm.

Vet Penalties: 1 to 2 penalties for each injury.

Total Penalties:

0 Gold, 1-2 Silver, 3-4 Bronze 5-8 Compl, 10+ Elim.

Award's

	Gold	Silver	Bronze	Completion
Speed Category:	SC1	SC2	SC3	
Thistle Award:	BTQ	BTF	STQ	STF	GTpart1	GT

Placing in Gated Ride:

– Competitive & Gated Ride VETTING SHEET –

Horse's Name: BALDER DASCALC

Log Book No: 0195

Type and Colour of Horse: chestnut arab X

Ride Date: 15.6.97

Blemish Details & Action Peculiarities to be completed by Rider & verified by Vet.

small scab near hind.
old swelling below hock
at hind.

Vet Time: 8:30

Heart Rates   Vet's Name

PRE-RIDE: Comments

1st MID-RIDE:

2nd MID-RIDE:

FINAL VETTING:

within 30 minutes

Vet Penalties:

Please state for cuts, sores and abrasions that are considered non minor.

In Competitive Rides only.

Vet Comments:

Vet Signature: Date:

Note: If a Horse is eliminated, score through the complete Vet Sheet and state the reason.

27

Understanding the Map

It goes without saying that you will have to learn how to read a map. You will need to know: how to find a grid reference (a specific point on a map using the numbers at the side and foot of your OS map); how to read contour lines which tell you how steep the hills are; to recognise feature 'on the ground'; and how such areas as woodlands, rivers, groups of buildings, even power lines of the National Grid, relate to the map in front of you. Time used in getting to know your way round maps is time well spent and quite fun, too. Every ordnance survey map has what is called a 'legend' printed alongside it. This is a list of the symbols you will find on the map and what they mean, as well as how to find a grid reference. Check them!

It can give you a great feeling of confidence when you know exactly where you are at any point on your riding route. It is surprising how many endurance riders are hopeless map-readers. Don't despair if you really can't manage the finer details of map-reading because the course you are riding is always marked by flags, tape, bio-degradable spray paint or lime. As a last resort, a bit of 'Indian scouting' can get you out of trouble. Hoofprints (preferably going the right way!) in soft ground or white horseshoe 'strike' marks on tarmac may just save the day. (*Warning* –make sure that you aren't tracking the local riding school out on a Sunday hack.)

> • *Hint: Even before you set out on the ride it is a good idea to orientate yourself at the venue in relation to your course map. Turn your map round so that it is actually pointing in the direction in which you will be leaving the start. Can you pick out any features around you that are shown on the map? Perhaps there is a very high hill, a wood or even a motorway cutting through the countryside. Look at the map, look at the features, and try to remember where they are in relation to the start and the course you are to ride. It may just help if you happen to get lost.*

Working out your Speed and Time

There will probably be a maximum time in which to complete the course. If you exceed this time you may be eliminated or the organisers may become fed up with waiting for you and go home! There may be a minimum time as well, so by going too fast you could be eliminated or incur penalties. Check your 'riding time' and mark this at various points on the map to give you an idea of your progress. Check the rules for the class you are entering to ensure you get it right. It is important to work out how long it will take you to cover a particular section.

Example: Suppose you have a ride of 15 miles from Start to Finish. You have checkpoints at 5 miles and 10 miles and you are aiming to travel at about 6 miles per hour (steady trotting, a bit of cantering). Using the speed chart, you can see how long it will take: 2 hours 30 minutes. Checkpoint 1 is 5 miles from the start so it will take 50 minutes. From the start to checkpoint 2, a total of 10 miles, it will have taken you a riding time of 1 hour and 40 minutes. Note down these times on your map and also those of 5 and 7 miles per hour. When you reach CP1 see how long it has taken you. If you are on time, well done, but if you are behind time you will need to make this up on the next section. You might even get too far behind the time for which you were aiming. Too far ahead of your time means that you will have plenty in hand to slow the pace a little but not so much that you end up behind time. This is part of the skill and challenge of riding the endurance trail.

this is part of a SPEED CHART for a ride of 15 MILES

this is how long it takes hr: min	this is how fast you ride mph
2:08	7.03 just about 7 mph
2:09	6.98
2:10	6.92
-	-
-	-
2:18	6.52
-	-
2:30	6.00 right on 6 mph
-	-
-	-
2:43	5.52
2:44	5.49 just about 5 1/2 mph
2.45	5.45

See page 79 for full time/mph figures.

Just to add to the problems of having to work out the time and speed of your ride, some societies give you a 'Gate Allowance'. This means that if there are more than a particular number of gates on a ride you are allowed an extra few minutes in which to finish, as the gates will increase the time it takes you to complete the mileage. You must take this into account when working out your finishing time.

> • **Hint**: *It is a good idea to set your watch to 12.00 at the start of the ride. This will give you your 'riding time' (e.g. if it is going to take you 45 minutes to get to a marked point on your map your watch will obviously read 12.45. This is much easier than starting your ride at, say, 11.43 and having to calculate 45 minutes from there).*

Course Markings

Your instructions should tell you how the course will be marked.
- FLAGS are used over open land
- TAPES are usually orange coloured and tied so that they catch the eye on trees, fences etc.,
- BIO-DEGRADABLE PAINT is sprayed on fences or gateposts or on the ground for direction.
- LIME (WHITE POWDER) is spread on the ground in the shape of an arrow to give direction, or across a forestry track to stop you going up that track.

Gates which need to be shut will probably have two bits of tape on the top rail. You *must* shut these gates. Gates which can be left open are usually marked with tape on the gate post – 'leave the gate'. If you are riding along a track and you are to take a turning to the left there should be two bits of tape close together warning you that there is a change of direction coming up. Then two tapes at the left hand turning will confirm the change.

Opening a gate (marked with tapes).

Tapes, markers and flags show you the way.

Tapes and markers (except flags over moorland) are not so frequent that you can literally ride from one to the other on the route. You must always look for markers. If you miss one and are unsure whether you are still on the right track go back to the last tape you saw and find where you are in relation to the map. It is not a good idea just to hope that by going on you will find another tape. Check. There will probably be other mileage classes running that day and their routes may cross of be part of your route. Make sure that you are following the right one.

Be warned, however: animals are inquisitive beings and like to chew, taste or even consume orange tape; and canes and white flags make useful scratching posts. Markers that were certainly there last night may

Change of direction; two tapes before the turning, one tape after.

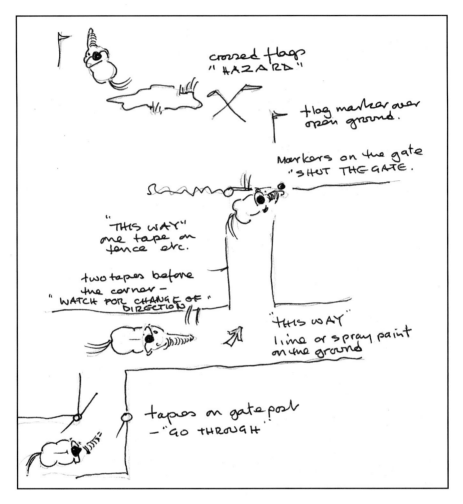

How markers are used.

have been 'lost' by the time that the first rider goes out. Regrettably there are also people who delight in causing as much havoc as possible and think it a bit of a laugh to move markers. This is why it is so important to constantly look at your map. Keep your wits about you. Notice landmarks so that you can pinpoint where you are. And don't just ride: look at and appreciate the countryside around you. It is likely that at times you will be going through areas which are usually not accessible to the public.

6

Your First Ride

The day of your first ride has arrived and it is now time to put all the theory into practice.

- You have studied your route map and worked out how long it will take you to ride to a given point. You have marked these on your map so that you won't arrive at the finish having to kill time, or in a fluster because you have gone too fast, have misjudged how the terrain or weather conditions would affect your speed.
- You have hi-lighted your 'talkround' instructions for quick reference.
- Your tack is clean and in good order.
- Your horse is soundly shod.
- You should have a vet sheet which will give you a time for vetting, probably a tack inspection time, and the time at which you will start the ride. Make sure that you have this with you, correctly filled in with any points you think that the vet should know.

When you arrive at the venue you should collect your number from the ride secretary and check that there are no last-minute changes to the

'The Venue'.

route, due, for example, to the weather. If there are changes, be sure to mark them on your map. be on time (even if things are running late with the organisers),There should be a marked area for tack inspection, another for the farrier and a trot-up area, where you will find the vet.

It is usual to go to the vet first.The time will be indicated on your vet sheet.Your pony should be wearing a bridle but no saddle and you will need to remove any rugs. Do not present your pony to the vet wearing boots or bandages.

The vet will need to listen to the horse's heart-beat using a stethoscope just behind the left elbow. Don't talk to the vet while he is trying to listen to the heart-beat. Try to be as quiet as possible, and don't engage in conversation with your friends, either. Often even the best vets have difficulty in hearing a horse's heart, and an accurate count can be vital.

The vet will note down any lumps and bumps which may be relevant. He will check that the horse's back and saddle are pain free as well as legs and mouth. He will note the general appearance. He will then ask you to trot the horse, in hand, to a marker 30 metres away and back again (remember to turn the horse away from you to save getting trampled and also to give the vet a clear view).This will enable him to check the animal's normal gait. If he isn't sure, he will ask you to trot the horse up again.All being well, you are fit to start.

The vetting area.

NB: In higher-mileage competitions the vets are very particular about soundness and irregularities of gait. Should there be any doubt, they will ask for a second trot-up. If they are still not happy they can ask for a third and final trot-up with another vet present. If the horse fails the third trot-up you are out, and eliminated from the ride. If you are not happy with the situation on the second trot-up, and think there may be a mistake, you must ask for a second vet to see the horse.This is usually done anyway, but if you did your third trot-up without asking for a second opinion and are vetted out you will have no appeal against the decision.

Hint: Before going to the vet it may be worth warming your horse up a little after the journey from home. Perhaps he is inclined to get a little stiff and it will save time and embarrassment if you present a horse whose gait you know the vet will not query.

While you are waiting your turn for the vet, make sure that you do not get too close to other strange horses. It would be a disaster to get kicked and not even start. It is sensible, saves time and frayed tempers, and is courteous to the vet, if you train your horse to stand still and squarely on all four legs; to allow himself to be examined without jumping all over the place and to trot willingly in hand at an even pace. Practice makes perfect. At an event is *not* the time to practice.

The Farriery Check

The farrier is not there to *shoe* your horse. His job is to check that the shoes are sound enough for the miles you are to cover; he may tighten up a clench. He would rather that you did not smarten up hooves with a liberal dressing of hoof oil before he has to pick them up, and he will also appreciate the fact that they have been cleaned out. Make sure that your horse is well shod a few days before the competition. If you lose a shoe on the ride you may be given penalty points unless you can get the shoe replaced before you present your mount to the vet at the finish. If you are unable or unwilling to get the horse shod by the farrier on call some societies now allow you to present for final vetting in a 'Shoof'. Check the rules.

Many otherwise good horses fail at this sport because shoes will not stay on or because the horse has brittle hooves and tender soles. The saying 'no foot no horse' must have been started by an ancient endurance rider!

Hint: If you loose a shoe on the ride and can pick it up, do so. At least there is a chance that it can be tacked on at the finish and so avoid penalties. Most ponies should have feet hard enough to cover several miles without damage if you keep off sharp stones and gravel. Pick your way and stay sound. Horses were not born with shoes, and sensible feeding practice and hoof care – including letting the horse run without shoes for part of the year – can ensure that you will never have a lame horse through the loss of a shoe.

There are hoof boots on the market well worth investing in – not just for endurance work.

The Tack Check

Before you present your horse, make sure that everything is in first-class order. The horse should be fully tacked up and you should be dressed ready for the ride. The tack inspector is not there to judge the *quality* of your tack but to check that it fits the horse and that it is safe. Make sure that your tack is clean, as it shows you take care of it, with no worn stitching on stirrup leathers or cracked and worn leather on reins or bridle. If you are using a martingale, check that you have rein-stops, that rubbers on safety-stirrups are sound and that straps are tucked into their keepers.

If you carry a stick it must be under 30" long (75cms). Your hat needs to be to the current standard laid down in the rules of whichever organisation you are riding with. Standards and requirements of dress vary from competition to competition and you may be required to carry a first aid kit. Always check the special requirements of each event.

You will certainly need a map-case to carry your map and talkround. These have a tendency to fly around and strangle you or to flap wildly and frighten the horse. Practise before the day – you could try and batten it down with a bit of elastic. You will be issued with a number bib so that you can easily be recognised at checkpoints and it may be possible to tuck your map-case behind it.

Always remember that the day of the ride is not the time for trying out new equipment.

The Start

Your horse's soundness has been checked, your tack has been passed and you have had plenty of time to check your route in advance. Orientate yourself by looking at your map once more, noting landmarks round you and how they relate to it. Make sure you are at the start in good time and ready to go at your given start time.

Riders are usually started at intervals of one minute, and probably two of you will go together. Your time will have finished when you cross back over the line. Make sure that your watch has the same time as the starter's clock, which is the time you will be clocked at, not what your watch says. This is known as 'synchronising'. Another method is to start your watch at 12.00 if you worked out 'riding time' and 'actual time' on your route map. Now is the moment to do that. Check your girth once more, and you are ready to go.

Make sure that your watch has the same time as the starter's clock.

The Ride

You will only learn how fast your walk, trot and steady canter are in miles per hour as you gain experience. Some horses put a lot of energy into their paces but all that effort is spent in going up and down not forwards and it may feel that a horse like this is covering the ground a lot faster than he actually is purely by the amount of energy going in to it. Practise when you exercise your horse by timing your ride. If you know it is a mile to your friend's house, trot steadily there at a consistent pace to see how long it takes. This will tell you how many miles per hour you are travelling. When working out speeds and times for competitions, bear in mind that hills and bad going can affect your speed. So you will need to study things like contour lines on the map and whether you are travelling on a tarmac lane or an unmade moorland track.

The weather will have an effect on your speed and performance. If it has been exceptionally rainy, the going underfoot could slow you down. In very hot weather, normally soft ground will dry out and some tracks could become rock hard. If it is very hot, both you and the horse can become dehydrated. This means losing body fluids by sweating and not being able to replace them quickly enough. At worst you can become confused: unable to make decisions and feeling dreadful. Take a high energy sports drink with you – it comes in squashy packs that slip into a pocket, or you may prefer to invest in a suitable holder that attaches to your saddle and takes a cyclist's drink bottle.

Your horse may lose so much fluid that when it comes to the final vetting he will not pass. A very fat pony, carrying too much weight and going too fast, will sweat profusely and be unable to replace the lost fluid. Always make sure that you allow the horse to drink as much as he wants whenever you have access to water. So if you have to cross a stream, for example, pause for a moment to see if he would like a drink.

Cold, wet, miserable weather can have its problems. Make sure that you have the right clothes for the weather. A lightweight waterproof tied to the back of your saddle may save you from getting thoroughly chilled and suffering from hypothermia – being so cold that you can't function properly.

However – you are going to have a good ride. You and your horse are well up to the mileage you have chosen; you can read your map and there are places for your horse to drink on the way; you made sure to have a good breakfast to keep your energy levels up – this is important – you have a high energy food in your pocket as well as a drink (not fizzy pop); you are wearing comfortable clothes, and your horse is comfortable in his as well.

During the ride it is your responsibility to make sure that the checkpoint steward has seen you and noted your number. These stewards are there both for safety reasons and to check that each rider has gone through. If they miss you, they will contact the venue and a search will be made. Never go home, even if you live just down the road, without making sure that the organisers know. Safety is very important when you are riding out like this – not only your safety but that of the people who might spend hours searching for somebody who just decided to drop out.

At checkpoints , refer back to your notes and check whether you are ahead or behind your planned time and adjust it accordingly in the next section.

Get off, to rest his back and stretch your legs.

You must always be on the lookout for markers and be able to decide just where you are on the map. Many markers are missed because riders are chatting away and not thinking about the job in hand, or enjoying a canter so much that they fail to spot double markers warning of a change of direction! *NB* This subject is covered under the heading of 'route marking'. Make sure that you have read it carefully.

A cheerful face will make somebody's day. This may be a tough competition but it doesn't mean that you can't smile and thank someone who is kind enough to open a gate for you, who slowed down in a car, or who may even be walking or cycling along enjoying the countryside. Be considerate.

Manners on the trail itself are also important. Don't fly past other riders without giving them warning. Don't crowd other riders. Don't dawdle along a narrow track when there are people wanting to come past. A steady, consistent pace will get you further faster than dashing off at a canter then walking then galloping along. It is a great temptation to shoot off when the going is really lovely. A steady pace, up and down hill, eats up the miles and saves energy. On longer rides you will appreciate getting off and jogging with your horse to stretch your legs and he will appreciate the weight off his back for a little while.

Problems on the Trail

If for any reason you are unable to go on, stay put and wait for the next rider to come along. Get him to report the situation to the next checkpoint: telling them your number and what the problem is. They in turn will relay the information to the start. This is why there are checkpoints. Don't take a short cut off the route or rescuers may not be able to find you. If you are unable to make your way slowly along to the next checkpoint, use the survival blanket from your first aid kit to keep you or your horse, whichever is the injured party, warm. You can get very cold if it is a bad day and you may have quite a wait before help arrives.

> *Hint: Consider what you might do in a variety of situations before they happen, so that you can meet problems head on with a clear idea of how you would cope. This exercise can take a lot of the fear out of things that may go wrong.*

The Crew

If you are lucky enough to have a crew, you will have arranged places on the route where they will meet you. They will have a drink for you and your horse; water to slosh him down; or a bucket and sponge to cool him. They will know how you are for time and whether you need

If you are lucky enough to have a crew... .

to push on or have plenty in hand. If it is really hot they might have a sponge of cold water for you to cool down with – one that hasn't already washed the horse. Most of all it is nice to see a familiar, encouraging face so remember to be nice to them!

The Finish

As you near the finish, check your time. Have you gone too slowly or have you left yourself plenty of time to steady down and start the cooling and unwinding process?

Make sure that the timekeeper has got your number and noted the time at which you arrived. You or your crew will probably be given a card with the time at which you should present your horse for final vetting. The time you have taken to complete the ride and the mileage covered will give the miles per hour at which you have travelled. (Penalty points for not keeping within the speed parameters are added to your veterinary penalties to give your final score.)

After you have crossed the finish line, jump off your horse and loosen the girth. Don't take the saddle off for a couple of minutes. If you were to pull it off right away, any damaged area would get its circulation back all at once, stressing capillaries and increasing the chances of a bad swelling. Find your crew – they should be at the finish line waiting for you. Throw a rug over your horse's quarters and offer him water but not food. Now you can remove the saddle, and if the horse is hot, cool him off by spongeing him down with cold water along the underside of his neck and between the back legs where you can see the main arteries. By cooling these arteries with water you will help to lower the pulse rate.

Walk him round and cool him again. If he spends a penny during this time it will help, too. You should eventually learn to use a stethoscope and be able to count the pulse so that you know exactly how well your horse is recovering. Keep an eye on the time and be ready to present to the vet promptly. Remember to feel the horse's ears, and if he gets cold rub them with a towel or between your hands. Make sure he has enough rugs to keep him from becoming chilled but not heating up. It is very easy to over-cool your horse and shoot the pulse rate up again. You will learn by experience how your particular horse's body copes with the stresses put upon it.

The best areas for cooling a horse.

Hint: *A calm crew and unfussy preparation of your horse before vetting will help keep his pulse-rate down. People rushing about in a hurry, with high, excited voices and short tempers, and over-enthusiastic sloshing and cooling, won't help a highly strung, excited horse to relax. Relaxing will help his pulse-rate to drop. A low pulse-rate means that your horse has come through the ride successfully. Some horses are naturally laid back and take the excitement of the ride in their stride, while others may take a season or two before they settle and vet well.*

Final vetting

Final vetting is usually 30 minutes after you cross the line. Always check the rules of the group with which you are competing and make sure you know what to do. Its purpose is to ensure that your horse has completed the ride in as good a condition as possible. There should be no cuts or bruises, and his back should be free of bumps; he should be happy for the vet to feel the saddle and girth areas to check this. His heart-rate should be under 64 beats per minute. This is the absolute top limit – a single beat over this and your horse will be 'spun' – vetted out. His state of dehydration will be tested. The vet will take a pinch of skin over the horse's shoulder and hold it for a few seconds. When he lets go, the time it takes to relax back into position tells him how much fluid the horse has lost and whether it is distressed. (Try this for yourself when the horse comes in from the field and see just how quickly the pinch of skin disappears.)

The 'pinch test.'

The vet will take the horse's pulse. Then you will have to trot him up to and around the marker as you did in the first vetting. This time, the vet will wait for one minute and then take the pulse again – which is known as the 'Ridgeway Test'. In a fit animal the pulse will go down on the second reading or it will stay the same. If it increases, it indicates that the animal is not as fit as he should be and that he is tired. You can incur penalty points for the number of beats over on the second reading and, of course, it must not be over 64. Legs, back and mouth are examined for injury and are penalised accordingly.

NB Different endurance societies have different systems of marking and grading. One day they may get together and make life easier for us all by having a single set of rules.

Take your horse to the vet with a rug on, as it is easy to get chilled if you have to wait around. You will have to take it off to trot up, of course, but put it back over his quarters while he is having to stand about.

If all has gone well, you will have completed the ride with no penalties. Endurance is the only sport where the veterinary condition of the horse is monitored so thoroughly, and the challenge is to bring you horse back in as fit a condition as possible. You should have finished the ride so that both you and the horse are willing and able to go a little further. The challenge is to improve on not just your performance out on the trail but to present your horse with a lower pulse-rate and in a better condition each time, bearing in mind the weather and terrain you have had to deal with. *It is a true test of horsemanship.*

Aftercare
Now you have almost finished for the day and are ready to go home. Your horse has had sufficient water and a small feed. (Had you allowed him to eat before he was vetted, it is quite possible that his heart-rate would have gone up a beat or two which might have been the difference between passing and failing.) You have prepared him for the journey home, bandaging his legs and rugging him up. Make sure he doesn't get chilled travelling in the trailer or box. Before you go, remember to return your number bib and collect your award and you vet sheet – not forgetting to thank the organisers for all their hard work.

Before leaving the venue, check that you haven't left anything behind and clear up waste hay and any droppings from around your vehicle.

Your horse will be glad to get back home for a good roll in his field and to rest and relax. If he is stabled, check that he has everything he needs, then leave him in peace and quiet.

The following day, check him over for any injury or swellings. His legs may have filled, especially if he has been stabled, but these will reduce

Your crew will be waiting for you at the finish.

as he walks around his field. He may be a little stiff and have lost some weight but he should be fine in a few days. No doubt the rider is a little stiff, too!

A good grooming will remove any sweat and muck left over from the previous day and will also give you a chance to check for tenderness on his legs or back. If his back is sore, you should try to work out why. Is the saddle causing a problem? Was your riding not as good as it might have been so that you rode heavily. Were you too active in the saddle or just too tired to think about it?

How well did you do in the event and were you satisfied with the way it all went? Can you see where you made mistakes. What have you learned by it all?

As your horse is having a day off, you will have plenty of time to give the tack a really good clean and check that nothing has been damaged. Time, too, to check out the crewing equipment and make sure that it is all together for your next ride.

Keep yourself and your pony fit enough so that your next endurance ride will be even easier for you both.

7

Crewing

Even if you haven't a horse to ride you can get a lot of enjoyment out of endurance riding by becoming a valued crew member.

Apart from low mileage and pleasure rides, the crew can be a crucial factor in the success of a horse and rider completing the ride. To start with all you need is a smile and to not mind getting wet from over-enthusiastic use of slosh bottles and sponges. It is useful, however, to be able to read a map, so that you can arrive at pre-arranged points on the course at the right time. You should be able to tell the rider whether she/he is on time, going too fast or too slow. It also helps to know the horse and his usual behaviour, so that you are more able to judge how he is reacting to any stress, and you can therefore be confident when holding him and handling him for the rider at vetting and crewing.

Riders sometimes get a little up-tight and say things that they regret afterwards, so a thick skin is a useful addition to the qualities of a crew member.

Your job is to help the rider before the ride begins: i.e. to get the horse vetted and ready to ride away; to meet the rider at points along the route with water for the horse if there is none available on the course; to offer refreshment to the rider. You are also needed to help at a halfway halt, if there is one; at the final vetting; and with the aftercare.

Many horses will not drink before 20 miles and then they will drink frequently. But do not try to force the horse to drink by sticking the bucket halfway up his face every time he stops. Your rider should make as much use as possible of water on the course – such as natural streams, drinking troughs etc. Many horses enjoy a slightly muddy puddle when they have refused the clean bucketful offered. Other horses will only drink from a bucket and then only familiar water.

Some horses just love sloppy sugar beet swimming in a bucket of water. This fluid contains some natural energy sources, and if the horse will take it – feed it to him! It will also help to disguise the fact the it is possibly not water from his own tap at home. On longer competitive

Natural sources of water along the route.

rides it may be possible to add electrolytes to the fluid for the replacement of salts, etc.

You will need quite a large amount of water unless you are sure that the horse can be persuaded to use natural sources on the route. A lot will be needed for cooling the horse. Make certain that you have water, buckets, sponges and slosh bottles out before the rider arrives on the scene, and be sure that the rider can see you as he/she comes in. If there is time, sponge the sweat from the horse's neck, inside the back legs and under the belly. Offer the rider the slosh bottle to tip water from poll to shoulder on the horse to cool him. Fabric softener plastic containers make good slosh bottles; they are robust and have sensible handles. Sometimes a crew member will walk up the route to meet the rider with a slosh bottle (so that the horse can then drink in peace at the crew point) or will hand a slosh bottle up to a rider so that he/she can cool the horse, throw down the bottle and keep moving.

'Sloshing'.

Do not pour water on the large muscles behind the saddle unless the horse is moving off immediately. On a horse that is standing around the water may cause stiffening or cramping.

Make sure that the rider has a drink – even if it is only a sip or two. Dehydration can happen inadvertently and can lead to errors of judgement as well as causing the rider to become quite ill in which case it could be difficult to replace the lost fluids. Riders tend to think of their horse's requirements and not their own, but the problems of dehydration in the rider might let the horse down. If it is really hot, the rider will appreciate a cold cloth or clean sponge for his/her face: try to resist using it for washing the horse down!

An extra sweater, waterproof or quilt will be needed in case the weather changes, so always make sure there is something available. If there is a mid-way vet check, you will have to prepare the horse by cooling and lowering the pulse to the required level before he can continue. Sponge the horse off with cold water in the 'cooling areas' of the larger arteries and scrape off with a sweatscraper. You will be

A cold, wet towel over the neck helps cooling.

surprised how instantly the water heats up on the horse, and you will therefore appreciate the necessity of this operation. A wet towel can be draped over the neck if it is a very hot day. This will retain moisture. You will need rugs to keep the quarters from getting chilled: even a New Zealand or waterproof rug if it is pouring with rain. At a halfway halt like this it is pleasant for the horse if you have a clean, dry girth and numnah ready for the second half of the ride. Make sure that there is no mud trapped under the girth area, which may cause soreness.

At any halfway halt make sure that you collect the time card from the time-keeper. This will you at what time you need to present the horse to the vet. Don't wait until the last seconds before telling your rider that you should be at the vet check. Keep and eye on the time and don't get flustered. Calm crewing can steady the horse, even if you are feeling hysterical inside because things aren't going to plan. Keep calm – don't panic!

Your rider may want you to run the horse up for the vet so make yourself familiar with the procedure. Otherwise, just be ready to whip the rugs on and off the horse at the right time.

Your efficient help can be the making of the ride: calm, cheerful, confident crewing is often the major factor in the horse and rider's successful completion.

NOTE TO THE RIDER

Your crew is there voluntarily, giving up their time to run after you. Be nice to them at all times!

Notes on More Advanced Crewing

As you become more involved with the sport you will realise the important part you have to play in the horse and rider 'team'. Your attitude towards both horse and rider will be the decisive factor in your success as a 'crew'.

Your rider will rely on you to be at the right place at the right time with the right information. You will learn to judge how your horse and rider are performing and whether they need more back-up in the next few miles or should be left to run on. Eventually you will be able to advise and guide your rider through the ride as well as knowing just how quickly the horse's heart-rate is coming down before the vetting. Your judgement will see them through.

On long, hard rides, when weather, terrain and stress have taken their toll on the horse, the use of electrolytes can play an essential role. (They are not necessary on short rides and should be used only in accordance with the instructions for each particular product.) They can be mixed with, and offered in, water. However, some have a particular taste and the horse may not only refuse to drink the water containing them but could be put off trying another bucket offered with fresh plain water. Horses can be very suspicious. Electrolytes could be slipped into sugar beet water if the horse is happy taking it. With a horse who needs electrolytes but refuses to take them in water, it is possible to put them directly into the mouth in a pre-mixed commercial 'gel' which comes in a syringe like a wormer. Experience endurance riders sometimes mix electrolytes with apple purée or syrup in a syringe. Use of these products is not necessary until you reach a higher level of competition and of competence in judging your horse's needs.

Massaging the muscles of the hind quarters can have very beneficial results by helping the horse to relax and therefore lowering the heart-rate.

Experienced crew members will have mastered the art of being able to use a stethoscope – sifting the sounds of the horse's insides from the sound of the heart and being able to count the beat. Heart monitors are available which give a digital read-out on a receiver (that looks like a watch) from a transmitter 'strap' held against the horse's side. These are expensive but become essential at higher levels of competition.

Suggested Equipment for Crewing
(you can manage with a lot less on short rides, of course)
Filled water-containers (5 gallon containers are too heavy to carry safely so look for something smaller that will take about half this quantity).
Never underestimate the amount of water you need.
Separate buckets for drinking and washing
Sponges
Sweatscraper
Towels (one for horse and one for human)
First aid kit
Electrolytes
Sloppy, fresh sugar beet water
Slosh bottles (with a funnel for refilling)
Plastic crate/box (so that bottles etc., can stand upright safely in a crew vehicle)
Stethoscope
Rugs – thermal, cooler and NZ depending on the weather
Headcollar and rope
Spare numnah, girth, stirrup leathers, reins
Spare clothing for rider
Drink and refreshment for rider
Your copy of map and ride instructions
Watch (set at the same time as your rider's)
Hoofpick
Penknife
Thermos of hot water (If it is a very cool day this can take the chill off washing down water)

8

Improving Your Skills

On the Ground

It helps if your horse is taught to stand still and quietly to be handled by the vet. The importance of this soon becomes obvious when you see the way in which some horses behave. If the vet has to examine a lot of horses in a short time he will appreciate one who, thanks to your efforts, stands quietly to have his heart-rate taken with the stethoscope and is not alarmed by the vet looking in his mouth and checking his back and legs. The farrier will also bless you for a horse who willingly lifts each foot at a touch and doesn't send him flying with a well aimed kick. Time spent at home practising is not time wasted.

The way in which some horses behave'.

The horse should also trot nicely in hand. You should neither have to drag him along nor be dragged by him. Hold your right hand a few inches down the rope or reins beneath the horse's chin and keep the surplus from trailing by holding it in your left hand. Do *not* wrap a lead-rope or reins around your hand. Give a little tug on the reins and a click or 'trot on!' of encouragement, then move forward, without looking back at the horse. If you trot, so should he. The vet can't see if your horse is sound if all he does is drag back and refuse to move on willingly. Practise every time you have to lead him so that he will do as you ask. Do not forget to turn the horse away from you as you go round the marker. If you pull the horse towards you he will almost certainly tread on your toes and you will obstruct the view of the vet. Don't hang on so tightly to the horse that you pull his head round, it makes it hard for the vet to judge correctness of the movement. Teach the horse to know the words 'trot on' and 'whoa'. Teach him to follow obediently in hand

Hanging on too tightly.   *The correct way.*

so that you can get off and jog alongside or take the lead over bad ground when you will need to have more than just a few inches of rein.

When it comes to crewing, either out on the trail or at the finish, it helps if the horse is used to being washed and sponged. Most become used to it and appreciate it when they are hot and sticky.

NOTE: The day of the ride isn't an ideal moment to try washing your horse's back legs for the first time.

On the Trail

It is worth repeating that good manners from both horse and rider are essential. Bad, uncontrolled riding, cantering on roads and general inconsideration to other users of the countryside give the riders and the sport in general a bad name. Many of the places where you ride are used by others - walkers, bikers - and they have as much right to be

Keep to the edges of fields.

there as you do. Always give fair warning that you want to come past, and don't assume that they know you are there. It is all too easy for people to think that endurance riders just rush from one place to another without thought or care.

Remember the Country Code and shut the gates. Be careful if you have to go through stock; sheep and cattle are only too glad of an excuse to rush wildly about and hurt themselves, and endurance riders passing their field can provide just the right invitation. If you are asked in the ride instructions to keep to the edges of fields because of crops, remember to do so. It may look like grass to you but it is still a crop; deep and wet ground poaches easily, hoof marks will still be there weeks later. Organisers of rides have to do a lot of persuading at times to obtain permission to go through certain areas, and careless or thoughtless riding will result in their never being able to use that route again. Don't forget to smile and say 'hello' to people you meet or 'thank you' to anyone opening a gate.

Consideration towards others also includes other competitors. If you are riding a slow horse on a narrow track, try to move on – or over – so that faster riders can get past. If you are wanting to pass other riders, make sure that they know you are there by calling out that you want to come by. Don't just race past: you may spook a nervous horse or you could well get kicked. On the subject of kicking, remember always to give other horses plenty of room and don't ride so closely to somebody's tail that you tread on the horse's heels.

Don't let the pressure of competition get in the way of sportsmanship or good manners.

Gates

You should be able to open and close a gate from horseback: though some-times it is quicker to get off and do it. Whichever way, make sure that your horse will stand still for you to mount. If you need to use a tussock of grass, a big stone or a gate to help you mount, he must learn to stand quietly. (It is good manners to wait for somebody who has opened or shut the gate to remount before you ride off.) Even if a friend has to help by holding your horse's bridle while you get on, your horse will eventually learn his manners.

Making use of a natural 'mounting block'.

Gates are there to stop stock from escaping, so always make sure that the gate is fastened securely. Ride organisers should check that there are no really bad gates for you to cope with, and they quite often arrange with the landowners to leave gates open for the duration of the ride. Check the markers so that you know which gates you can leave open and which must be shut. If you are riding in a group it is only fair to take turns at doing the gates.

Balance

It goes without saying that a good rider achieves better results than a bad rider and this is never truer than in endurance. It is easier for your horse to carry you if you ride in balance and rhythm with him. Don't ride too high at the trot – let it flow. Check your stirrup length, you won't have to jump anything on the ride, and short stirrups can cause a lot of stress and fatigue on ankle, knee and hip joints. It will become easier for you to ride well, because if you don't it will hurt. It has been said that pain is a great teacher, and once both you and your horse are going comfortably together it means that you are riding well.

By leaning forward up steep hills you can free the horse's quarters and help him move forwards more easily – even if you have to hold on to a piece of mane while you do so. If you are riding downhill, ease your weight back a little and give you horse enough rein to allow him to see where he is going.

Knowing your Horse

The whole sport of endurance riding is based on a good working relationship between you and your horse. You have to know his capabilities. You need to know what is 'normal' for him, so that you can tell if he becomes stressed, as well as how far and how fast he can go. You will become a better horseman the longer you spend in his company and on his back. He must have confidence in you as well as you having confidence in him. Together, you will have a lot of fun and find out the meaning of true horsemanship.

9
Trekking

The word 'trekking' now seems to describe a string of bored ponies trailing along at a minimum pace, carrying novices or non-riders who are probably unsuitably dressed and wishing that they were doing something else. However, it can also inspire a burning ambition to learn to ride and to become a real horseman.

Trekking centres offer a range of activities from riding in a 'nose-to-tail' novice string to more adventurous, faster rides, taking your own or a hired horse on a pre-arranged, carefully planned ride of several days. You can find suitable establishments through advertisements in magazines, lists from the BHS or Ponies of Britain, or by personal recommendation – the latter is best.

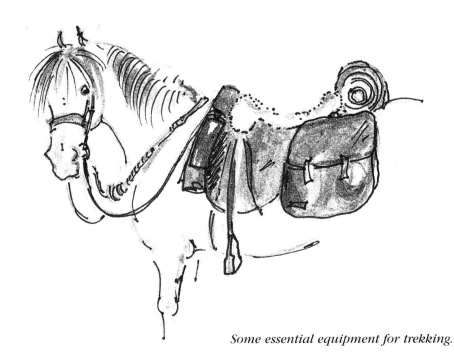

Some essential equipment for trekking.

Your own Trek

Finding your own way, working how long it will take, knowing what equipment to carry and having a willing, handy, fit horse to share it with is a real journey of adventure.

Britain offers a maze of bridleways, many of which are linked together to make long distance riding routes. There are various publications available either from the BHS or the local Tourist Board which list places offering bed and breakfast for horses and riders. These will give you ideas for routes – or you can work out your own, using Ordnance Survey maps. Remember, though, that because a path is marked on the map it doesn't mean that (a) you can physically negotiate it and (b) that bridlepaths can change into footpaths. Local bridleway groups will give you advice. Lots of research is needed before you embark on a lengthy trek of this sort.

Preparation for your trek is similar to that for endurance in as much as you and your horse must be fit enough to cover the distance planned for each day. Your tack and equipment must fit, be comfortable and suitable. Don't forget to take spares – at least a stirrup leather and a pair of reins.

> **Hint:** *Leather bootlaces are very strong and once tied tend to stay tied. you can use one to mend just about anything:*
>
> • *If horse treads on reins and snaps bridle: tie one end of the bootlace to the bit-ring. Now thread it up over the horse's head through whatever keepers and buckles remain of your bridle, holding it all in place, and down to the other bit-ring. Adjust and tie off into the bit-ring.*
>
> • *Snapped stirrup leathe: whip a damp lace tightly over the two overlapping broken ends.*
>
> • *Laces are also very good for tying your coat and extra gear to the D-rings of your saddle.*

Your usual tack will be quite suitable, but make sure that your saddle has sufficient D-rings. Modern saddles usually have them in the front and possibly on one side. You will need them on both sides to balance your pack. Needless to say, your saddle must fit your horse, allowing freedom of shoulder movement and distributing your weight as evenly as possible over his back. It must be comfortable, as you are going to be in it a long time – even though you will be getting off and walking

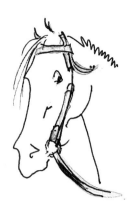

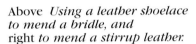

Above *Using a leather shoelace to mend a bridle, and* right *to mend a stirrup leather.*

occasionally. You could invest in a 'seat saver' either of sheepskin or a 'gel pad' type. These slip over the seat of your saddle and are attached by tape or elastic.

You will need a headcollar under your bridle and you should carry a rope, attached to the saddle or around the horse's neck. Combination bridles are ideal for trekking as you need only unclip the bit hanger from the D-rings on the bridle to have a headcollar; if you are thinking of more than one trekking adventure it may well be a good thing in which to invest. They come in BioThane – a plastic-coated, washable material, very strong and in lots of colours – or webbing.

You will need spare clothes, equipment, food etc. even if you are not camping out, so use saddle bags that go each side behind the saddle, or a cantle bag which attaches to the back of the saddle.

Whichever way you decide to carry your baggage, before you set off make sure that your horse is used to carrying a strange load safely. The weight must be evenly distributed and must not bang about.

If you are planning to camp out you will have to consider the extra equipment needed and decide how you are going to carry it. A pack pony may seen like a good idea in theory but leading the extra horse can be a trial and a hazard. Better to think logically about equipment that can be shared and try to distribute the extra weight between you.

Safety
You must consider the safety aspect of your trek:

Safety of route: Amount of roadwork and traffic-related problems.

Natural hazards of terrain – boggy ground; stones which could cause injury; very steep slopes; impenetrable woodland; river crossings.

Safety of your mount: He should be comfortable, sound and sensible to ride and should be willing to be tied up.

Safety of equipment: Everything must fit and be in sound condition. Make sure that you can easily put up any tent you carry.

Suitability of companions: You should all be capable horsemen and women, and your horses should all get along so that they can be safely turned out together at night. There should be no fewer than four in your group; in the event of trouble, one person can go for help; one can act as horse-holder and one can remain with the injured rider. As well as safety in numbers there is safety in good pre-planning.

Six is the maximum number for riding as a group safely on the road. You should all be able to work as a team and each should know how to read a map.

Leave a route-plan with a parent or other responsible person in case of emergency.

Suggested pack list for trekking
– *not camping out at night*

Change of clothes
Waterproof clothing
Basic toiletries
First aid kit (includes survival blanket
  but possibly more items than
  carried in the endurance
  'bum bag')
Torch
Whistle
Maps for route
Compass
Paper
Pen
Penknife
Horse brush
Hoofpick

A few more items of equipment are needed for trekking.

High-energy food and drink
   for rider (emergency pack)
Food for horse and rider
Emergency repair items
'Shoof' or similar

– camping out at night
Tent
Sleeping bag
Cooking equipment
Food supplies for horse and rider

If you are planning your own trek where there are places to accommo-
date horses and riders, you will need to be sure that fencing is safe, that
there is ample water available for your horse, and that feed can be pro-
vided by the establishment. If not, you will have to make prior arrange-
ments for feed to be delivered. Even good doers will need a bit of energy replacement at the end of the day. If you are only out for a couple of
days, it may be possible to carry a coarse-mix ration but it does add to
the weight.

   When planning your riding day, a good average mileage would be
about 20 miles. Don't try to go too far. Leave yourself time to cover the
miles you have planned. Break the riding up with stops for grazing
(horses and riders) and spend time walking on foot to ease your

muscles and your horse's back. A good lunch-stop where saddles can be removed and the horses given a chance to graze and roll will set you both up for the second half of your day's journey. You will find the ride more enjoyable if you vary the pace – a good walk, jog or trot or even a canter if packs and saddle bags stay steady. Unending walking is tiring and boring for everyone. Don't forget to look around you and appreciate the places where you ride. At least one of you should keep a 'Trek Diary'. Commonsense, good horsemanship and sensible planning will help to make your trek safe but still a journey of adventure.

10
The Duke of Edinburgh's Award

The Award is designed to encourage a spirit of adventure and discovery. Each venture demands enterprise and imagination in its concept, with forethought, careful attention to detail, and organisational ability in its preparation. Preparatory training both in theory and practise leads on to safety in journeying in a chosen environment. The shared responsibility for the venture will encourage leadership within the group, self reliance, and co-operation, together with a determination to complete the plan. A 'Reflective Report' is required on the purpose of the venture.

Careful attention to detail.

The venture will help you to:
- Demonstrate enterprise through travelling with a purpose.
- Work as part of a team as a group effort.

- Develop leadership skills.
- Recognise the needs of others and be able to adapt.
- Make decisions and accept the consequences.
- Plan and execute a task.
- Respond to the challenge – especially environmental influences.
- Enjoy and appreciate the countryside.
- Reflect on personal performance.

Full particulars of the scheme, how it works and how to enter can be obtained from the Award Office, Gulliver House, Madeira Walk, Windsor, Berks. SL4 1EU telephone 01753 727400. Notes from their *Expeditions on Horseback* leaflet will give you some idea of what you should consider when planning such a venture.

Bronze Award
14 to 25 year-olds. Two days with one night camp.
This must involve travelling for a minimum of four hours each day in addition to setting up camp, route planning and horsecare. Routes should always avoid villages and towns.

Bronze Award participants should use lanes, tracks and bridleways and have a minimum of Pony Club 'C' standard with a knowledge of tethering and picketing; competence in the well-being of the horse; recognition of dangerous going and knowledge of what action should be taken in the event of accident to horse or rider. There should be at least one practice journey to correspond as closely as possible to the Bronze expedition.

Silver Award
16 to 25 year-olds. Three days with two night camps.
This must involve travelling for a minimum of five hours each day in addition to the setting-up camp, etc., using lanes tracks and bridleways. Pony Club 'C' or 'C Plus'. There should be a minimum of two practice journeys or the Bronze Award plus one other.

Gold Award
16 to 25 year-olds. Four days with three night camps.
Minimum of six hours travelling each day, etc., using tracks as previously described plus riding in wild or open country. (Specified areas include Cheviots, Border, Dartmoor and other similar areas of which there are 32 in all). Riders to be Pony Club 'B' standard. There should be a minimum of three practice expeditions – one of Bronze, two of Silver.

Horses must get on with each other at night.

Horse expeditions present a special challenge, especially Silver and Gold Awards, and participants should be aware of the advised standards of expertise. All should be involved in riding in rural surroundings on a regular basis. Thought needs to be given to a suitable horse, for example: a horse may not get on with others in the party, giving problems when turned out at night. He will need to be fit for the expedition, especially at Silver and Gold level when riding conditions will be more demanding.

Requirements for mounted expeditions are similar to those for all other ventures in that participants are expected to be dependent on their own resources as much as possible, though horses may present particular problems. The country in which the venture takes place should be unfamiliar to the participants, but a small amount of reconnoitring may take place to ensure that tracks etc., can be negotiated on horseback and that permissions from landowners for overnight camps sought.

All participants must be totally self-sufficient and free from any adult intervention. Each venture has a supervisor who is responsible for the safety of the participants and has sufficient qualification or experience to ensure the welfare of the horses. Ventures are monitored at specific checkpoints along the route – but not so that they destroy the group's sense of self reliance. A horsebox or trailer can be placed at a strategic location in case of lameness, injury etc., and telephone numbers of the local vet and farrier should be noted. Normal camping equipment which would be used in a walking expedition (that is, lightweight tent and light stove) can be set up in advance, together with items required for the horse.

In case you fail to reach your destination you must take sleeping bags and other emergency equipment, which might include a tent to cover all riders – crowded in – or bivvy bags, as well as spare clothing, first aid equipment and rations as in the previous chapter on trekking.

All riders must wear approved hats, but, otherwise, dress should just be suitable and safe.

These awards, which should not be undertaken lightly, can stretch your knowledge of horsemanship and of yourself. By taking on the challenge of endurance riding you discover more about the need for fitness in horse and rider; become adept at riding unknown country with the aid of a map within the limits of a specified time; and, in planning even a simple trek, your organisational, map-reading and leadership qualities are put to the test. All these can lead on to the successful completion of a Duke of Edinburgh's Award, and they will also increase your skills as a horsemaster. Through horses, you will learn more about yourself.

Further Notes and Glossary

Aftercare	Looking after your mount after the ride.
Arteries	Tubes or vessels which carry the blood from the heart round the body. By cooling the large arteries along the sides and down the hind legs you can cool the blood, and therefore the horse, during crewing.
BERA	British Endurance Riding Association.
BioThane	Trade name of an extremely strong webbing with a plastic coating.
Bivvy Bag	A sleeping type bag with good thermal and weather protection which can be used without a tent.
Bum Bag	A small bag or pouch on a belt worn round the waist to take essentials: e.g. first aid kit.
Checkpoints	Points along the route where stewards (who are usually in radio contact with the ride HQ) check that you are safe and on the correct route. This is a safety measure to ensure that nobody gets lost.
Chilling	This happens when the horse has become too cold too quickly, through over-cooling. To compensate, his heart-rate increases and he may visibly shiver. The efficient use of a stethoscope, to keep a check on the heart-rate while cooling, can prevent this. A Heart Rate Monitor (HRM) is even better.
Contour Lines	Lines marked on the Ordnance Survey maps, usually at 10-metre vertical intervals. The lines indicate the gradient of the land: e.g. the closer the lines the steeper the hill.
Cooling	The major part of crewing can be the cooling of the cooling of the horse to reduce his heart-rate which is determined by the amount of energy he has

expounded on the ride, creating heat. Cooling by sponging cold water on the main arteries near the surface: e.g down the hind legs, helps to bring the temperature down quickly. Other areas to cool are the neck, shoulders and belly. Wipe the water off as it becomes warmer, and keep up the process until you reach near the minimum heart-rate required.

Country Code   This is a code outlining how you should behave when in he countryside. One of the aims of the Pony Club in running endurance riding activities is to give young people and their families the opportunity to have fun and enjoy the countryside, and to promote environmental awareness.

Crew/Crewing   The team behind the rider. Crewing is essential to to the smooth riding and final presentation of the horse. It should ensure that everything is to hand when needed and that you have a cool head to cope with your rider!

Dehydration   Condition caused by the loss of fluids and salts from the body. Usually due to heat. It is a real problem with horses who won't drink enough water to replace the loss of fluids and salts through sweating during exercise. Cautious and correct use of electrolytes can help overcome this. Many horses willingly drink sugar beet water which has a natural source of energy. Riders can suffer dehydration, too, and crews should make certain that their riders drink during the ride. Isotonic sports drinks help a lot.

SUGAR BEET WATER

Dress	See the Pony Club book *Correct Dress for Riders* for guidance. Each Branch of the Pony Club should ensure that its members are aware of the require ments. However, dress at most endurance events out side Pony Club is fairly casual. The correct standard headgear, recommended by the societies, along with sensible footwear and comfortable clothing suitable for the discipline, with well-fitting tack for the horse, will suffice.
Duke of Edinburgh's Award	An award for young people between 14 and 25 years of age who undertake character-building enter- prises. It has three categories: bronze, silver and gold.
EHPS	Endurance Horse and Pony Society.
Electrolytes	Electrolytes are referred to as 'tissue salts'. They are essential for the regulation of body fluids to prevent dehydration, and can be given to horses in water, gels, etc, to replace the salts lost through sweating during hard exercise. But they are a specialised product and should only be used as and when recommended: e.g they must only be given to a horse already drinking well and not to one who is refusing to drink.
Energy	Energy is essential for the satisfactory completion of the ride by the horse and rider. It comes in the form of correct food and drink which is stored by the body and used up in relation to activity. Riders can use high energy food bars and drinks to sustain them. High

energy feed for the horse should be used according to his temperament and the demands (i.e. distance travelled) made on his energy.

Equi-Boots A trade name for boots designed to fit around and under the hoof, protecting the foot in the absence of a shoe. Also 'Shoof' and 'Easi-Boot'.

Farrier Your farrier is the endurance rider's best and most valued friend, taking care of you horse's feet and shoes for safe miles on the trail. He will be able to fit your horse with the correct shoes for endurance riding, which have more bearing surface and are longer at the heels.

Farriery Check On most rides the condition of the horse's shoes are checked to see that they are safe and sound for the mileage you are undertaking.

Feed The old saying 'feed according to work and temperament' holds good when you are working out requirements for endurance riding. Overfeeding can be as dangerous as underfeeding. Knowing your particular horse's needs comes with experience. There is no substitute for good quality feed. Endurance horses need more forage (chop,hay) in the gut to retain moisture which in turn lessens the risk of dehydration; and a feed giving a slow release of energy.

Fitness The fitness of both you and your horse will make or break your ride. Both of you must be fit for the mileage you are undertaking. Fitness in the horse can not be hurried, and hardening of the tendons and strengthening of muscles starts with boring walking not fast trotting. An unfit horse may well suffer strains and stress, leaving him unsuitable for future competition.

Footwear For Pony Club requirements see *Correct Dress for Riders*. Other societies insist that unless you are wearing footwear with a heel you must have cages fitted to your stirrups. Trainers and similar footwear (except specialist riding trainers which have heels, and which allow you to run or jog alongside your horse) are never suitable for riding. Avoid boots with slippery soles; they are dangerous if and when you are on foot over grassy hills. Long leather boots are not really suitable for endurance.

Gait   The pace at which a horse travels. Walk, trot and
        canter are standard in Britain although some horses
        'pace' – moving two legs on the same side instead of
        diagonally at the trot. If the horse has a naturally
        uneven gait you must mention it on your Vet Sheet
        (and hope that the vet accepts it as your horse's
        natural way of going and not as a sign of lameness!)

Gates   The ability to unfasten and fasten a gate will speed
        your ride. If the gate is to be closed(denoted by
        marker tapes tied to the top rail of the gate) make
        sure that you have fastened it securely.

Gate   Under some rules you may receive a 'gate allowance'
 Allowance if there are more than a certain number of gates on
            the route. This enables you still to ride at the designat-
            ed speed set for that class: e.g if your riding time is to
            be 2 hours to ride at 10 miles per hour and there is a
            gate allowance of 5 minutes you are allowed 2 hours
            and 5 minutes to ride the course at 10 miles per hour.

Going   Good or bad going can describe the condition of the
            ground over which you are travelling. Good going
            might be grassy tracks, bad going may be stony, deep
            or wet ground.

Grid   An OS has lines going from South to North
 Reference (Northings) and from West to East (Eastings). The lines
            have corresponding numbers marked at the side of
            the map going south to North and then the line at the
            bottom going West to East. Read the **Eastings** first

(the numbers going West to East) then the **Northings** (the numbers going from South to North). If you have trouble remembering which way round to read off the numbers, think of 'going along the hall and then up the stairs'. Where the two lines cross is the **Grid Reference**, which may be read as, say 670450. Each of the squares between the lines can be divided into ten. Supposing your point of reference is about half-way between 45 and 46 on the north/south line and a bit more on the east/west line – you could be more accurate and give the reference as 677455. A full size Ordnance Survey map will provide all this information as well as a key to the symbols (called the 'legend').

Heart-Rate Monitor	Also referred to as a 'pulse monitor', this is used for keeping a constant check on the horse's heart-rate while he is competing, and also at crewing. With a very small transmitter placed against the horse's skin, either under the saddle or in the girth area, the heart-rate can be detected and sent to a wrist-watch type receiver which provides a constant, visible readout. These instruments can be of great value at a high level of competition as a guide to the horse's performance under pressure; his fitness; and his recovery rate during crewing.
Heart-rate	The rate at which the heart beats. At rest it is between 35–45 beats per minute. A rate of more than 64 on presentation to the vet at the end of the ride incurs elimination.
Holds	As in 'Vet Holds'. A period of time during a long ride when there is a compulsory hold or rest-time for the horse.
Horsemanship	Endurance riding is a test of horsemanship: to be able to ride skilfully and with consideration for the horse, and by correct feeding and fittening, finish the ride in a condition 'fit to continue'. The Pony Club aims to promote a high standard of horsemanship, particularly in developing an awareness of fitness in both horse and rider.
Hypothermia	A condition caused by severe chilling. The body temperature drops dangerously and the body slowly ceases to function. It can happen, for example, when

	horse and rider are not properly prepared for bad weather.
In hand	Trotting up for the vet when leading the horse with a bridle or headcollar, is known as leading 'in hand'.

Kestrel	The second of the four categories of Pony Club Rides: 10 miles at a speed between 6.5 and 8 miles per hour.
Log Book	If you intend to ride in classes of 20 miles or over your horse will need to be registered with one of the endurance societies. One log book per horse covers you to compete in all societies. It contains particulars of your horse – its registration number, a mileage record card and your vet sheet from each ride and is a 'safety net' for the horse. Should your horse frequently fail through lameness, etc, the vet may advise you not to compete for a while. It also helps to record your horse's progress and provides a long-term record of his competition history. Once the horse is registered you will not be allowed to start the ride without pro ducing your log book.
Map case	You will need this clear plastic, waterproof case to hold your map and ride instructions so that you can easily refer to them during the ride. It is worn around the rider's neck.
Markers	Coloured tape (usually orange), attached to a fence, tree, etc, to confirm your route, warning of a change of direction and indicating gates to be shut. Over

open ground, flags may be used. Lime powder or bio-degradable spray paint are an alternative. The method to be used will be indicated on your ride instructions.

Massage   Massage techniques can be used to relax the horse and thereby help to reduce the heart-rate.

Merlin   This is the first of the four Pony Club categories of ride. It is for 5 miles at a speed of 5.5 to 8 miles per hour. Two rides at each level must be completed satis-factorily and officially recorded. The four rides must be attained in sequence (Merlin, Kestrel, Osprey and Eagle). Badges and certificates are awarded.

Neoprene   A soft rubber-type fabric used for boots and for covering a girth or breastplate.

Number Bib   All riders wear a number bib so that they can be iden-tified at checkpoints etc.

Obesity   Term used to describe fatness and overweight.

Ordnance Survey	The whole of Britain has been surveyed and mapped by the Ordnance Survey, who produce numbered maps for each area. These show all ground features: e.g roads, buildings, rivers – and indicate ground heights with contour lines at 10-metre vertical intervals.
Osprey	The third of the Pony Club Ride categories: 20 miles to be ridden between 6.5 and 8 miles per hour.
Passing	Always give adequate warning that you would like to pass other riders so that they can move over and you can pass in safety.
Penalties	In the final vetting you may receive penalties for bruising, over-reaching and soreness, as well as dehydration. Time penalties may also be incurred if you go below or above the permitted time for the particular ride.
Pinch Test	By taking a pinch of skin on the horse's neck or shoulder and seeing how long the fold of skin takes to resume its normal state you can tell the amount of dehydration he is suffering. This is a usual part of the final vetting and may incur penalties.
Pleasure Ride	A ride of up top twenty miles, but usually a lot shorter, with a generous time allowance at maximum speed to protect the horse. Before and after the ride you are unlikely to have to do more than a 'trot up' rather than a vetting.
Pulse	The measured beat or throb of the heart and arteries. It can be felt where an artery is near the surface of the skin: e.g under the jaw bone or behind the horse's elbow. Knowing how and where to feel and read a pulse on your horse can help you to judge his

	recovery rate. You should know his usual resting pulse rate. Using a stethoscope just behind his elbow on the near side will enable you to hear his heart-rate.
Quietness	A quiet, calm, unflustered crew will help a horse through his vetting more easily than a noisy, chaotic one.
Quiltie	Australia's famous long distance ride.
Race Ride	For experienced, well qualified riders only. Usually over 50 miles with a mass start. The first one home presenting sound with a heart-rate of 64 or or under is the winner. For any distance over 50 miles there is usually at least one Vet Gate or Hold approximately 20 or 25 miles apart. You may present your horse as soon as possible with a heart-rate under 64, after which the clock is stopped and you may rest for anything from 10 to 40 minutes, depending on the rules of the day. The clock starts again at the time at which you should leave. This can be a tactical race and tends to be very competitive.
Ridgeway Test	At the final vetting you horse's pulse-rate will be taken. You will be asked to run the horse up in hand, and one minute later the pulse will be taken again. This will indicate the fitness and recovery rate of your horse. The pulse-rate should drop on the second count on a fit horse and should increase on a tired one. It is also referred to as the 'Minute Test'. As it is not carried out in all endurance societies, check the rules.
Riding Time	Time taken to complete the ride but excluding any time at a compulsory hold or rest period.
Rugs	You will need a thermal type rug that wicks away moisture while keeping the horse warm. If you use a sweat rug, put a light rug over it. For cold, wet days while waiting for final vetting, a New Zealand rug is a useful addition – particularly over the hind quarters, to stop muscles stiffening.
SERC	Scottish Endurance Riding Club
Saddles	Once you are competing in rides over 50 miles your GP saddle is unlikely to be suitable because of the pressures put on your horse's back from the length of time that you are on board and the miles covered. Thanks to new concepts in saddle design a variety of

specialist saddles are available for the serious endurance rider. Whichever saddle you use, it MUST FIT and be comfortable for both you and the horse. Remember that the horse will change shape with increase and decrease of fitness.

Saddle Sore
On the horse – a sore patch caused by an ill-fitting saddle or a foreign body: e.g. grit – between saddle and horse.
On the rider – a sore seat. A sheepskin or specialist seat-saver over your saddle can help prevent this. Good riding helps, too!

Slosh
Water from a plastic bottle given by the crew, possibly on the run, to tip over the horse's neck and shoulders to cool him.

Speed Charts
Available from Endurance Societies. These give you every distance from 1 to 50 miles; and the time and speed in miles per hour needed to cover that distance. They save a lot of effort in working out projected riding times and are very accurate.

Speed Parameters
Minimum and maximum speeds between which you must complete the ride.

Sponge
Essential equipment for crewing. Soaked in water it is used to cool the horse during and after the ride. Riders can also make use of any available natural

water on the trail to cool the horse by carrying a sponge on a string clipped to their saddles.

Spun

A term used to indicate that a horse has failed the veterinary examination.

Start Time

Time indicated on your ride instructions or vet sheet at which you must be ready to start your ride. In some competitions the clock is started at the stated time whether or not you are ready. Check the rules.

Stethoscope

Used for listening to the horse's heartbeat by placing the diaphragm of the instrument against the horse's side just behind the elbow on the near side.

Stress

This can be suffered by the horse in travelling to and from the ride; by the excitement of the event; by not being fit enough for the ride and having too little energy in reserve; or from not having sufficient liquid and becoming dehydrated.

Sugar beet

A good addition to the feed. Soaked beet pulp helps the horse's gut to retain fluid by damping down the feed. Beet pulp water contains a little sugar and can boost energy levels if offered during and after a ride.

Survival Kit

A collection of items (carried in a 'bum bag') which are considered to be essential by the endurance societies. A basic kit should contain an elasticated (horse) bandage, a triangular bandage, wound dressing, hoof pick, survival blanket (foil blanket), bivvy bag, whistle, glucose tablets and rider identification card.

Swellings

After a ride it is quite possible for your horse to have slightly swollen joints. Bandaging or the use of

cooling packs, followed the next day by gentle exer
cise, usually reduces these swellings. If they are on the
back they may be caused by poorly fitting saddles or
bad riding.

Sweating   The horse will sweat when working, excited, hot or
stressed. Salts and body fluids are lost by sweating and
need to be replaced to reduce dehydration. Some
horses sweat more than others.

Tailing   This tactic is used by experienced riders when they
have to dismount in very hilly or mountainous country, so that the horse can climb freely without a
weight on his back. The rider usually has an extra long
rein, or may unclip one side from the bridle, walking
behind the horse with the rein in one hand holding
on to the tail, and getting a 'lift' up the hill.

Talkround   Also referred to as 'Ride Instructions'. These written
instructions correspond to the route marked on your
map.

Terrain   The type of ground over which you are riding. It
could be very steep, rocky or boggy, and you would
have to ride at a slower than average pace. You may
be given a 'Terrain Allowance' if the organisers think
that you will have difficulty in making the maximum
time allowed.

Tevis   Reputedly the hardest 100-mile-in-one-day event in
world and a forerunner of today's great endurance
rides. Organised by the American Endurance Rides
Conference.

Timekeeper	The official at the start and finish who clocks you out and in, keeping a record of your time so that your award/speed can be worked out.
Trek Diary	Diary of events, special features, points of interest, written on a daily basis whilst trekking. A compulsory part of the Duke of Edinburgh's Award syllabus.
Trot Up	Pleasure riders will probably only have to 'trot up' their horses for the vet before and after the ride rather than having a full vetting and may be allowed to present the horse tacked up. Check the rules.
Tying-up	This condition is also known as azoturia or 'Monday morning sickness'. It is usually brought on by too much stress too soon in the ride, with a sudden build-up of lactic acid in the muscles, producing intense cramp. The acid build-up may be caused by too high protein food being retained in the horse's system. Unfortunately it is a common problem in endurance horses, and a satisfactory reason for it or cure has yet to be found.
Vaccination	At some big rides, or where horses are to be stabled overnight or starting on racecourses, etc, it may be compulsory for your horse to have an up-to-date vaccination certificate.
Vet Sheet	At rides of higher distance than a Pleasure Ride you are likely to have a Vet Sheet. This will show details of your horse's age, height, sex etc, and will give you your vet time and a start time. It will also ask for any injuries or peculiarities of gait that you want to bring to the vet's attention. He in turn will record comments to remind himself of the horse's condition when he, or another vet, sees it at the finish; and the horse's starting and finishing heart-rate; also whether he has completed or failed the ride. A copy of your Vet Sheet must be kept in your horse's Log Book.
Vetted Out	Term used to describe failing the veterinary examination before, during or after the event. Your horse may be vetted out before the ride if the vet does not think him sound or fit enough to compete. At a vet hold or at the end of the ride the horse must be sound, with a heart-rate of 64 or under, or he will be vetted out or 'spun'.
Venue	The place from where the ride starts.

hr:min	mph
2:00	7.50
2:01	7.44
2:02	7.38
2:03	7.32
2:04	7.26
2:05	7.20
2:06	7.14
2:07	7.09
2:08	7.03
2:09	6.98
2:10	6.92
2:11	6.87
2:12	6.82
2:13	6.77
2:14	6.72
2:15	6.67
2:16	6.62
2:17	6.57
2:18	6.52
2:19	6.47
2:20	6.43
2:21	6.38
2:22	6.34
2:23	6.29
2:24	6.25
2:25	6.21
2:26	6.16
2:27	6.12
2:28	6.08
2:29	6.04
2:30	6.00
2:31	5.96
2:32	5.92
2:33	5.88
2:34	5.84
2:35	5.81
2:36	5.77
2:37	5.73
2:38	5.70
2:39	5.66
2:40	5.63
2:41	5.59
2:42	5.56
2:43	5.52
2:44	5.49
2:45	5.45
2:46	5.42
2:47	5.39
2:48	5.36
2:49	5.33
2:50	5.29
2:51	5.26
2:52	5.23
2:53	5.20
2:54	5.17
2:55	5.14
2:56	5.11
2:57	5.08
2:58	5.06
2:59	5.03
hr:min	mph

*Time/mph figures
for speed chart*

Index